A SLICE OF LIFE . . .

A Collection of Poems

A SLICE OF LIFE . . .

A Collection of Poems

written by
Janet Anne Lowther

ARTHUR H. STOCKWELL LTD
Torrs Park, Ilfracombe, Devon, EX34 8BA
Established 1898
www.ahstockwell.co.uk

ISBN 978-0-7223-4975-5
*Printed in Great Britain by
Arthur H. Stockwell Ltd
Torrs Park   Ilfracombe
Devon EX34 8BA*

AND A LITTLE BIT OF THAT . . .

Pills and potions, creams and lotions
all promise to make us feel great,
apart from the pills we take when we're ill
and feeling a bit of a state.
Stuff to take for aches and pains,
creams to rub on to dry skin,
some camouflage for varicose veins
and lotions to soothe a sore chin.
Tablets to take for hair long and lush,
or so all the adverts claim,
so why is mine like a hawthorn bush
that has just been caught in the rain?
Be warned: some concoctions are risky
and these are the ones to reject,
but others can make you feel frisky
(what a brilliant side effect!).
If a man can walk into a chemist
with something resembling a worm(!),
a pharmacist can suggest a plan
that will make his worm nice and firm.
He then walks out with his head held high
and everything nicely in place.
The pills and potions will set things in motion
and put a big smile on his face!

A LOST LOVE

I just dread the onset of evening
And the hurt that builds in my heart,
For I know that when I try to sleep
That's when the teardrops start.

Each night I spend hugging my pillow,
Pretending you are still here with me,
And I weep for you, the love I've lost –
You were more than the world to me.

When daybreak comes I face the world
And appear to be coping well,
But then the dreaded evening comes
And another night of hell!

Time hasn't really healed the pain
Or helped me with my fears,
For every night instead of sleep
I spend the night in tears.

A CHANCE TO DANCE

To dance, they say,
is good for the soul.
Uplifting and lively,
it suits young and old,
so pump up the volume
when you get the chance,
stop what you're doing
and get up and dance.
You can dance in the kitchen,
dance up the stairs,
dance in the street,
just dance anywhere.
If you want private lessons,
or to dance en masse,
meet like-minded people,
why not try a dance class?

AND SO TO BED . . . EVENTUALLY!

When your booster cushion has lost its boost,
and you struggle to get off your seat,
you need a chair that will rise and recline,
to get you back on your feet.
If the only way you can manage the stairs
is to drag yourself up on all fours,
a stairlift could just be the answer,
and would save your knees getting sore!
So now for a shower, or maybe a bath –
simple if you have a good hoist.
It just whips you in and whips you out,
not surprisingly leaving you moist!
This is where a good fan comes in
which will dry you from head to toe,
but better still if you have a man,
why not let him have a go?
If all this activity has tired you out
and at last you are ready for bed,
a good idea is an adjustable one,
with a lever to raise your head.
The positions are endless
if you press the right knob –
find the position you like
and you've done a great job!

AUTUMN GLORY

Majestic trees
stage an autumn show –
spectacular foliage
gives a golden glow.

Ribbons of colour
suspended in fronds
of russet red
and burnished bronze.

Glints of gold
mingle with yellow –
colours that clash
or subtle and mellow.

Enjoy while you can
this dazzling display
before leaves begin to fall
and it all fades away.

AN OPEN-AND-SHUT CASE

I hope that I can be recycled
when I'm finally 'over the hill',
and made into something useful –
a suitcase might just fit the bill.

A classy case that really stands out
and owned by someone who cares –
someone who wants to travel the world
and preferably a nice millionaire!

I could be at the ready night and day,
excited at the thought of a trip,
quite easily led, and laid on the bed
while my owner unfastens my zip!

The packing will only take minutes,
which will probably suit any man,
but being a case with plenty of space
he can stuff in as much as he can!

But when all my travels are over
and I've been everywhere on the planet,
I'll be slung on the tip, with a well-worn zip,
a lovely old suitcase called Janet!

BOTTOMS UP!

If you just sit around
you are bound to succumb
to a very common problem
well known as 'numb bum'.

You probably won't realise
till you get off your chair,
and may just for a while
think your backside's not there.

Your legs start to buckle
and knees start to bend;
hubby, quick as a flash,
tries to grab your rear end.

As he rubs your numb bum
and the feeling comes back
that's just what you needed
to make it lovely and slack!

YOUR WORLD

Your eyes look so sad
as you gaze into space –
you don't know my name
or remember my face.

I tell you I love you
and silently pray
that you will respond
and have something to say.

When you hear music –
a favourite old song –
you sing a few words,
but it never lasts long.

At times you seem anxious
in quite a strange mood.
I try and reassure you,
but you seem so confused.

What of the future –
our time left to share?
Although you're still with me
your mind is elsewhere.

You are like a prisoner
locked in a dark cell,
the walls without windows –
a true living hell.

WHEN YOUR WILLPOWER WILTS

When your lettuce leaf is really limp
and your broccoli has finally gone off,
the fruit in the bowl has passed its best
and you're desperate for a good scoff.

Fish and chips are sadly forbidden,
I am trying my best to eat less,
the biscuits are really well hidden
and I'm feeling a right bloody mess!

But willpower wilts at times like this
when your tummy really starts to rumble;
you suddenly realise how much you miss
fresh cream on a rhubarb crumble!

FAT CHANCE!

All fired up to get myself fit,
sick of being flabby and fat,
decided to start by doing the splits
right here on the living-room mat.

Preparing myself to take the plunge,
I was really quite anxious to start.
I just had to make an eye-watering lunge
and land with my legs wide apart!

Landed face down, it didn't seem right,
spreadeagled and a little bit fraught,
maybe because my skirt was too tight
or my legs were a little bit short!

FLOOR BORED!

We really enjoy our line-dancing classes,
young and old, lads and lasses.
Without exception there's got to be one
that causes hassle – obnoxious Ron!

He shuffles about in the middle of the floor –
he really thinks he looks good.
To me he is just a bloody big bore
and dances as if made of wood.

He's sarky and rude to Alison,
who teaches us every new dance.
Will mutter and moan to little Joan
whenever he gets the chance.

I wish he would take a 'chill pill'
and put a smile on that miserable face;
but better still, if he choked on the pill
the world would be a happier place!

GOOD GOLLY – A BIG BLOW-UP DOLLY!

This 'dolly bird' is not what you think –
she won't wiggle her boobs
or pour you a drink.
No fishnet tights
or glimpses of thigh –
this little 'dolly'
is quiet and shy.
A real contortionist
when you get her to bed,
you can bend her and stretch her,
stand her on her head.
So don't be disappointed
at the charms she may lack –
just think of your heart
and that poor aching back!

HAPPY NEW YEAR

Christmas is over,
New Year is in view,
tree starting to droop
and the baubles askew.
Lights started flickering
and finally flicked off(!),
relatives start bickering,
hubby has a bad cough.
Cards tumbling over
from the dresser top shelf,
and someone has trodden
on my favourite elf!
Can't wait to take the decs down
and stick back in the loft,
must eat the choccy Santas
before they go soft!
Christmas is lovely
with family and friends,
but if I am honest
I'm always glad when it ends.

Happy New Year.

BETTY

There was a young lady called Betty,
who had hair like uncooked spaghetti!
It was so long and matted
she could cut it and plait it
and anchor her boat in the jetty.

HAVE FAITH

Please do not fear tomorrow,
but relish life today.
When all around is sorrow,
have faith, be brave and say
some days you will have sad days,
your tears like falling rain;
but as the dark clouds rise
you will dry your eyes
and you will smile again.

A KNEES-UP

Hubby has had a knee replaced
which has really worked a treat;
he seemed to be going really well
and his scar was nice and neat!

But now he is looking all po-faced
and totally racked with pain,
he needs another knee replaced
and must go through it all again.

But hopefully that will do the trick
and be the end of his creaking knee,
he can then get rid of his walking stick
and, at last, be completely pain-free!

NICE PUSSY

My friend has a lovely big pussy,
a fabulous ball of fluff!
She just loves to be stroked,
not so keen on being poked,
and will nip if you get a bit rough!

KEEP DANCING

Don't ever stop dancing –
it's good for the soul.
Line dance or Latin,
it's all rock 'n' roll!

Try the Argentine tango,
Charleston or jive –
whichever you choose,
you deserve a high five.

MEMORIES

Woods full of snowdrops
and bluebells galore,
a grotto and gardens
for us to explore.

Rambling orchards
full of peaches and pears –
wonderful times
when we had no cares.

But the lovely old house
that once was our home
will always hold memories
wherever we roam.

Those were the days
when the sun always shone.
We were young and carefree –
sadly those days are gone.

MAGIC MOMENTS

Hedgerows and woodlands
in blossom and leaf –
a truly breathtaking sight.
Dormant creatures awake
from beneath,
emerging from darkness to light.

Blackbirds and thrushes
chorus at dawn,
doing their courtship display.
Out in the fields the lambs
just newborn
enjoying the sun as they play.

Carpets of colour
in gardens just zing!
Daffodils, tulips and crocus –
hoping that heralds
a wonderful spring
with the beauty of nature in focus.

POOR OLD 'MOO'

Muriel is my sister-in-law
and quite a jolly lass.
She is very, very happy
when there's whisky in her glass.

She was quite a party animal,
who loved to dance and sing,
would leap upon the tables
and do the Highland fling.

Sadly, like the rest of us,
slowing down as we get older,
Muriel tripped and fell one day
and broke her arm and shoulder.

Now poor old 'moo' sits in her chair,
cheesed off and wracked with pain,
but knows that given half a chance
she would do it all again.

OUT OF STEP

After years of wearing ill-fitting shoes
my feet are now totally wrecked –
arthritis and gout, some toes that stick out,
and a few, for some reason, erect!

The Doctor suggested specially made shoes,
and examined and measured my feet.
Sadly, no more Louboutin, or Jimmy Choos,
so elegant, so glamorous and neat.

Instead I must settle for shoes big and wide,
which conjure up an image of flippers,
huge strips of Velcro down either side
and insoles like well-frozen kippers!

I'm sure there's a way that I could enhance
this footwear that looks odd and funny,
but if I can walk, and I can still dance,
that will make me one big, happy bunny!

PENSIONED OFF!

Mention the word pension,
makes me feel really old.
Dread the thought of bungalows,
warden-controlled –
those quaint little homes
that all look the same.
Each one has a number,
but seldom a name.
On tiny front lawns
with freshly cut grass
sit weird plastic gnomes
that seem to grin as you pass.
A few random plants
in a lopsided pot
propped up near the wall
in a nice sunny spot.
Every front door
a strange shade of blue –
net-curtain-draped windows
obscure the view.
I could wear a beige mac
and brown lace-up shoes,
play bingo every night,
have an afternoon snooze!
I cannot help but think
it's the step before heaven.
I may just give it a try –
when I reach ninety-seven!

REMEMBER ME

I have made
this little poppy
especially for you.
The leaves, I know,
are slightly limp,
the petals all askew!
So wear it with pride,
wear it with love,
for those who have died
and look down from above.

RUBBER DOLLY

Derek is a very dear friend,
but has not got a wife.
I could not really comprehend
him alone for the rest of his life,
so I bought him a blow-up dolly,
thinking he would be thrilled,
but this weird-looking object
was slightly overfilled.
She certainly looked bloated
and not what he had in mind.

This little dolly
is not what you think –
she won't wiggle her boobs
as she pours you a drink.
The girl in your dreams
is really quite shy –
no fishnet tights
or glimpses of thigh.
She's not a contortionist
if you take her to bed,
she won't tickle your feet
or stand on her head.
Sadly not the real thing,
and some charms
she may lack,
but think of your heart
and that poor aching back!

DREAM ON, JOHN

There was an old man called John,
as fruity as a freshly made scone.
He would eye up the lasses
in his old steamed-up glasses
and dream of the days now long gone.

SO SPECIAL

Some things in life are so special,
and being a granny is one –
someone to love who loves you in return
and brings you such laughter and fun.
I treasure every moment spent with them,
seeing life through those innocent eyes,
when the whole world around them's exciting
and every new day's a surprise.
As long as I live I will love them
and help them as much as I can.
I pray they will always be happy
and make me a very proud gran.

SKIN-DEEP

Do I really need Botox?
My mirror says yes –
a crumpled old face
that's frankly a mess.

I could have a facelift
to peel back the years,
have saggy skin from my chin
hoisted up to my ears.

Would love to donate
spare flab from my hips,
which in turn may inflate
my poor wizened lips!

But would I be happy?
There is no need to ask
if my face just looked frozen
like a weird plastic mask!

It all sounds so frightening
and just a bit rash.
My skin may need tightening,
but I'm saving my cash!

BILLY GOAT ROUGH?

Our parents kept goats
when we were quite young,
some nannies and a billy –
he was quite highly strung!
The nannies were canny –
I am sure there were five,
milked every morning
by myself and brother Clive.
At the crack of dawn
before going to school,
we headed for the shed
with a pail and little stool.
If you are near to a nanny,
it will nibble your hair,
chew holes in your clothes
and dribble everywhere!
We would scuttle off to school
in a real dishevelled state;
most days we were in trouble,
mainly for being too late.
Now the billy was a bully,
would chase me everywhere
and butt me up the backside –
he didn't really care!
But one particular day,
as I ran towards the gate,
my brother shouted, "Jump, lass –
before it is too late."
With billy right behind me –
that goat was rally manic! –
I had to do something very quick,
I was really in a panic.
With a mighty leap, I cleared the gate
and landed in a heap.
Why oh why did our parents keep
goats instead of sheep?

THAT'S LIFE!

Long blonde hair,
sparkling blue eyes,
a nice flat tummy
and well-toned thighs.

Years have passed;
things have changed,
all my bits
now rearranged.

Hair is grey,
wiry and thin,
cellulite thighs
and a double chin!

Arthritic hips,
walk with a stoop,
thin, puckered lips
and boobs that droop.

This once so chic
heart-stopping 'dolly'
now has a stick
and tartan shopping trolley.

THE HOLE STORY

A gang of workmen turned up today
equipped to dig a big hole,
somewhere between my garden gate
and a nearby electrical pole.

Stood at the ready, a few burly blokes
accompanied by gaffer Big Bob.
Quick as a flash they whip out their tools
and are keen to get on with the job.

Really just doing what men do the best –
digging a massive big hole,
proudly putting their tools to the test
like moles that are out of control!

The men work well when the boss is about,
but when he is out of sight
they lean on their shovels, have a drag on a fag
and hope it will soon be night.

Unfinished holes appear everywhere,
causing havoc, and traffic to queue.
Nobody quite knows why they are there,
but it gives the blokes something to do!

WELL PLASTERED

Sheila's got a plaster on –
she's badly hurt her knee.
She fell down in the kitchen
while making a cup of tea.
Slowly limping to her desk,
sat down to her work.
She crossed her legs
and they stuck like pegs
and she really felt a berk!
Cos as she tried to leave her desk
her legs were stuck like glue.
She stood there lurching
back and forth
as drunkards often do.
But once she'd prised her legs apart
she really felt relief,
cos falling down with plaited legs
could really cause some grief!
The moral of this story is
To avoid a real disaster
Just be careful what you hurt
And where you stick your plaster!

WHAT'S UP, DOC?

Went to the Doctor's
earlier this week,
feeling a bit of a state.
The girl in reception
announced with a shriek,
"The Doctor is waiting –
you're late!"
Shuffling across
the waiting-room floor,
quickly knocked
on the Doctor's door.
"Come in," he said.
"Please take a seat.
How can I help you today?"
My legs were so swollen
my knees wouldn't meet –
there was nothing much
else I could say.
"Leap on to the bed,"
he said with a smile.
Could this be my lucky day?
Having not had a leap
for quite a while,
this was certainly
no time for play!
Clambered on to the bed
with the aid of a chair,
I did as was bid
and stuck my legs in the air.
He examined my legs –
no messing about –
legs that resembled old trees.
"I'm pleased to say
you do not have gout,
but you could have
Dutch elm disease!"

YOUR WORLD

Your eyes seem so sad
as you gaze into space –
you don't know my name
or remember my face.

Each day is a challenge,
not life as we planned,
so unpredictable,
so hard to understand.

The future's uncertain
for the time we can share –
you are with me in person,
but your mind is elsewhere.

Although like a prisoner
in a dark lonely place,
you're the one that I love
and could never replace.

A SCARECROW SHOW

A gruesome old witch on a broomstick
in flight above the WI
was startled by a ghost, wrapped herself round a post,
putting paid to her spooky night fly!

If this lady had gone to Specsavers
she would not be struggling to see;
but lost without specs, and with arms outstretched,
she smashed right into a tree.

One scarecrow I love is the gardener
complete with his compost and spade –
Monty Don at his best, having a well-earned rest,
and the one that my granddaughter made!

Outside her front door a sexy young thing
surprised neighbours by taking a shower.
With wine at the ready, she won't be too steady
if she stays there for more than an hour.

Adorning our lawn is a lovely pink pig –
she is one you just cannot ignore.
This one you can't eat, cos she's not made of meat,
But stuffed to the gills with old straw!

The scarecrows we know were the stars of the show
and really brought our village to life,
which just goes to prove that the things that we love
are the simpler things in life!

BUCKET LIST

Some people I know have a bucket list,
doing things that are crazy or cool,
like flinging themselves from the top of a cliff
just to dive into a deep icy pool!

Hurtling head first from an aeroplane,
hell-bent on a parachute jump,
arms down by their side, legs open wide
as they meet Mother Earth with a bump!

Give hang-gliding a try, if you want to fly
and spend hours just floating in space,
but one thing on their list not to be missed
is to abseil down a sheer rock face.

Flying high, I confess, does not impress,
or perhaps I am not very brave!
But I feel safe and sound down here on the ground,
where I know I can still misbehave!

THE JOURNEY OF LIFE

We all take the same journey
on a long but winding track,
where the only way is forward
and no way of turning back.

When you find life is a struggle
and the journey seems too long,
a friend or loved one beside you
will guide, and keep you strong.

In your youth you chase rainbows,
seek your own pot of gold,
spread your wings, try different things,
never dream of growing old.

You eventually reach a crossroads
and assess your journey so far.
Have you climbed the highest mountain?
Have you caught a falling star?

But these things are not important
in order for you to succeed.
To be loved, be happy and healthy
are all you will ever need.

NHS!

I was just getting over a bad bout of flu,
but still did not feel very great.
Staggering out of bed, early hours, for the loo
I felt I was not walking straight.

Somehow I lost my way back to bed,
flaked out as I walked past the bath,
cracking my ribs and bumping my head –
I was laid there just folded in half!

Hubby, ever helpful, was doing his best,
especially as dawn was just breaking,
yawning his head off, and stood in his vest
and alarmed at the noise I was making.

The doctors were busy – a paramedic came out
and found me sprawled on the settee.
Kindly he said he would soon sort me out,
then promptly got down on his knees.

He checked me all over, according to plan –
what he thought was just anyone's guess!
So a heartfelt thanks to this lovely man
and all the staff of our great NHS.

DEAR DAD

As Father's Day approaches,
sons and daughters everywhere
are probably buying presents
to show him that they care.

But really all that's needed
and to truly make his day
is to tell him that you love him –
the most important words to say.

For the day you lose your father,
and there's just an empty space,
you can no longer tell him
that you love him, face-to-face.